William H. Taylor

The School Laws of Vermont in Force April 1, A.D. 1893

William H. Taylor

The School Laws of Vermont in Force April 1, A.D. 1893

ISBN/EAN: 9783337779450

Printed in Europe, USA, Canada, Australia, Japan

Cover: Foto ©Suzi / pixelio.de

More available books at **www.hansebooks.com**

THE

SCHOOL LAWS

OF

VERMONT

IN FORCE

APRIL 1. A D. 1893

Compiled under an Act of the Legislature

BY

WILLIAM H. TAYLOR,

MEMBER OF THE VERMONT BAR.

BURLINGTON:
THE FREE PRESS ASSOCIATION, PRINTERS AND BINDERS.
1893.

PREFACE.

By authority of No. 108, Acts of 1892, I was appointed by His Excellency the Governor to compile the school laws of the State in force April 1st, 1893. I have the honor to submit herewith the result of my labors.

The work in hand being a compilation and not a revision of the school laws, the exact language of the statutes has been preserved.

The school laws were revised and codified by the Legislature of 1888; consequently the act of that year has been taken as a basis for this compilation, and the several amendatory acts passed by subsequent Legislatures have been applied thereto. Sections in addition to existing laws have been distributed throughout the appropriate chapters of the work.

Proper references have been made below each section, so that the accuracy of the compilation can be readily tested by reference to the original enactments. Suggestions thrown into the body of the compilation have been enclosed in brackets to distinguish them from the language of the statutes.

Part I. contains the general provisions of the school law. With the exception of Chapter V. and a few sections of Chapter IX., it contains the law both for schools under the town system and for those exempted from the provisions of the town system act. Part II. contains the parts of the old school law continued in force for school districts not abolished by No. 20. Acts of 1892. In Part III. will be found several topics of interest and value to school officers and the public generally.

The sections in the several chapters are numbered consecutively for convenience of reference.

It has been my endeavor to simplify the work and thereby to render the problem of construing the school laws less difficult for school officers.

WILLIAM H. TAYLOR.

Hardwick, Vt., Feb. 6, 1893.

TABLE OF CONTENTS.

PART I.

PART II.

PART III.

PART I.

General Provisions of the Laws Relating to Public Instruction.

CHAPTER I.

SUPERINTENDENT OF EDUCATION.

SECTION 1. The General Assembly shall elect, at each biennial session, a superintendent of education, who shall have general supervision of the public schools of the State, and devote his whole time to the duties of his office. A vacancy in said office shall be filled by the governor.

1888, No. 9, sec. 1.

SEC. 2. The superintendent of education shall receive an annual salary of two thousand dollars, and his necessary expenses when traveling on official business, to an amount not exceeding six hundred dollars.

1888, No. 9, sec. 2.

SEC. 3. He shall have an office in the state house, and may employ a clerk to assist in statistical and other office work at an annual compensation not exceeding four hundred dollars.

1888, No. 9, sec. 3.

SEC. 4. He shall be supplied with stationery for official use, and his payments for postage and for freight and express charges necessarily made in connection with his official duties, shall be allowed him in the settlement of his account.

1888, No. 9, sec. 4.

SEC. 5.   The superintendent of education shall hold a teachers' institute in each county during each biennial term, and may hold additional institutes if in his judgment advisable; but not more than two institutes shall be held in any county during a biennial term.   An institute shall not continue more than four days.

1888, No. 9, sec. 5.

SEC. 6.   If the superintendent of education is unable to be present at a teachers' institute, he may direct the supervisor of schools [examiner of teachers] of any [the] county to conduct such institute.

1888, No. 9, sec. 6, amended by 1890, No. 5, sec. 8.

SEC. 7.   In every teachers' institute especial attention shall be given to the training of teachers in methods of instruction; and the superintendent of education may employ persons specially skilled in such work to aid in an institute when he deems it advisable so to do.

1888, No. 9, sec. 7.

SEC. 8.   The entire expense of a teachers' institute shall not exceed thirty dollars for each day such institute is in session, and the same shall be paid by the superintendent of education, and be received by him from the state.

1888, No. 9, sec. 8.

SEC. 9.   The superintendent of education shall, on occasions other than the holding of institutes, visit each county annually, and as many towns in each county as practicable, deliver lectures upon educational subjects, confer with and advise school officers and teachers, and investigate the condition of schools.

1888, No. 9, sec. 9.

SEC. 10.   The superintendent of education shall present to the General Assembly, on the first day of each biennial session, a report for the preceding two years, which shall contain an account of his official doings, a statement of the condition of the schools and of the expenditure of the school money, and such suggestions for the improvement of schools as he deems proper.

1888, No. 9, sec. 10.

SEC. 11.   Not more than four thousand copies of such report shall be printed.   Each supervisor of the schools [examiner of teachers] shall receive twenty copies.   Members of the General Assembly, town clerks, district clerks, and principals of graded, union and high schools shall each receive one copy.   The superintendent of education shall make such distribution and shall send the copies, except those for supervisors of schools [examiners of teachers] and members of the General Assembly, to the town clerks, who shall deliver them to the persons entitled thereto.

1888, No. 9, sec. 11.

SEC. 12. The superintendent of education shall, at the end of every three months, file with the auditor an itemized account of his expenses verified by his oath; and as soon as the same can be examined, he shall receive an order on the treasurer for the amount found due him on such account, and for one-fourth of his annual salary.

1888, No. 9, sec. 12.

CHAPTER II.

EXAMINER OF TEACHERS AND TOWN SUPERINTENDENT.

EXAMINER OF TEACHERS.

SECTION 13. At each biennial session of the Legislature, or as soon thereafter as may be, the State superintendent of education and the governor shall appoint one man in each county, who shall be a resident of the same, and who shall be styled examiner of teachers. A vacancy in the office of examiner shall be filled by the State superintendent and the governor.

1890, No. 5, sec. 3.

SEC. 14. Said examiner shall, under the direction of the State superintendent of education, make all necessary arrangements for holding teachers' institutes in his county as required by law; take measures to secure the attendance of teachers at the same; give assistance at such institute; and furnish such statistical information as may be required.

1890, No. 5, sec. 8.

SEC. 15. The examiner shall receive four dollars per day for time actually spent in the discharge of the duties of his office, and his necessary expenses, which shall not exceed two dollars a day, and expenditures for postage and stationery for official use; and such examiner shall, at the end of every six months, file with the State auditor an itemized account of his expenses, verified by his oath, and as soon as the same can be examined and approved, the State auditor shall transmit to him an order on the State treasurer for the amount due him on such account.

1890, No. 5, sec. 9.

SEC. 16. Whenever the examiner shall, in the judgment of the State superintendent, prove himself unfit for the duties required of him, or his services become unprofitable, he may be removed by the State superintendent and governor, and a successor appointed in his place.

1890, No. 5, sec. 10.

SEC. 17. The examiner shall, in the month of June next preceding each biennial session of the General Assembly, send to the superintendent of education a report of his work as examiner, with such suggestions as he may desire to make.

1890, No. 5, sec. 11.

TOWN SUPERINTENDENT.

SEC. 18. The board of school directors shall, on or before the first day of April in each year appoint a town superintendent of schools whose duties shall be the same as now required of town superintendents, but whose compensation shall be fixed by said directors.

1892, No. 20. sec. 12.

SEC. 19. The term of office of a town superintendent shall begin on the first day of April next after his appointment and continue for one year and until a successor is chosen.

R. L. sec. 458, amended by 1892, No. 20, sec. 12.

SEC. 20. It shall be the duty of the town superintendent of schools to visit the schools of the town for which he shall have been appointed, at least once each term, and oftener as the school board may direct. He shall note the methods of instruction and government, inform himself of the progress of the pupils, and give such advice to the teachers as may be needed.

1892, No. 21, sec. 25.

SEC. 21. He shall, when visiting a school, observe the condition of the school house, outbuildings and grounds, see if the school is properly supplied with maps, reference books and apparatus, and ascertain if all the pupils are provided with necessary text books, and make such recommendations to the school directors as to the conditions and needs of the schools as he deems best and necessary.

1892, No. 21, sec. 26.

Sec. 22. The town superintendent of each town shall have power to dismiss any teacher who, in his judgment, has proved himself incompetent; such dismissal shall be given to such teacher in writing, and such teacher shall receive pay *pro rata* to the time of dismissal.

1890, No. 5, sec. 15.

Sec. 23. In towns having a graded school district chartered by a special act of the Legislature, the directors or committee of the graded school district, and those of the town district, may unite in the election of a town superintendent; said directors or committee shall together fix the compensation of such superintendent, determine the proportion that the graded school district and the town district respectively shall pay of the sum so fixed, such proportion to be paid out of the treasury of their respective districts.

1892, No. 21, sec. 27.

SUPERINTENDENTS OF TWO OR MORE TOWNS.

Sec. 24. Any two or more towns, the aggregate number of schools in all of which is not more than sixty nor less than thirty, may, by vote of the school directors of the several towns, unite for the purpose of employing a superintendent of schools, under the provisions of this act.

1892, No. 21, sec. 28.

Sec. 25. When such a union has been effected as provided in this act, the directors whose duty it is to elect a superintendent of schools, shall form a joint committee, and for the purposes of this act, said joint committee shall be held to be the agents of the several towns forming the union. Said committee shall meet annually, in the month of March, on the second Tuesday after the annual town meeting, at some convenient place agreed upon, at 10 o'clock in the forenoon, and shall organize by choosing from their number a chairman and secretary. Said committee, when organized, shall choose by ballot a superintendent of schools ; determine the relative amount of service to be performed by him in each of the towns, fix upon his salary and apportion the amount thereof to be paid by each town. But said salary shall not exceed in dollars a greater number than one-third the total number of weeks of school of all the schools of the town forming the union.

1892, No. 21, sec. 29.

Sec. 26. Graded schools acting under special charter may avail themselves of the privilege of section twenty-nine of this act, [section twenty-five of this compilation], if its directors or committee so elect, and said school shall be considered a town for that purpose, and each department of said graded schools shall be counted a school for the provisions of said section.

1892, No. 21, sec. 30.

SEC. 27. When a superintendent shall have been chosen as provided in section twenty-eight of this act, [section twenty-four of this compilation], and the several towns shall have paid the apportionment as therein provided, the school directors or committee of the several towns shall present a bill to the auditor of accounts for a sum equal to twenty per cent of the town apportionment of the salary of such superintendent and the auditor of accounts shall draw his order on the State treasurer in favor of such town for said sum.

1892, No. 21, sec. 31.

CHAPTER III.

NORMAL SCHOOLS.

SECTION 28. The normal schools at Randolph, Johnson and Castleton are continued until August, A. D. 1900.

R. L. sec. 462, amended by 1888, No. 10, sec. 1.

SEC. 29. The State superintendent of education shall nominate and approve a principal teacher and a first assistant teacher for each normal school, and shall withdraw such approval when the interests of the school demand; and no person not so nominated, or the approval of whom is withdrawn, shall be employed as such principal or first assistant; but the principal may select his other assistants and provide for the discipline of the school.

R. L. sec. 463.

SEC. 30. There shall be two courses of study in a normal school and no more. Each course shall contain such branches as the trustees of the school and the State superintendent shall agree upon; but no foreign language, ancient or modern, shall be included therein. No study or subject not included in the established courses shall be taught in a normal school,

R. L. sec. 464.

SEC. 31. The State superintendent shall ascertain each term of half year whether the provisions of the preceding section have been complied with, and in case of non-compliance on the part of the school, or of the trustees or teachers thereof, shall withhold the certificates upon which the auditor of accounts is authorized to draw his order for the payment of moneys to such school.

R. L. sec. 465.

SEC. 32. The examination for admission to a normal school shall be controlled by the trustees of such school and the State superintendent. The examination for graduation shall be conducted by a board consisting of the State superintendent, the principal of the normal school, and a practical teacher who shall be annually appointed by the governor from the congressional district in which such school is located, and who shall receive four dollars a day and his traveling expenses while in the discharge of such duties. Such board shall attend and assist at such examination ; and shall grant certificates of graduation to all who pass the required examination in the first course or both courses, but may revoke said certificate upon cause shown.

R. L. sec. 466.

SEC. 33. Each town shall be entitled to one scholarship in a normal school, and a person appointed to a scholarship may attend either of the normal schools in this State at his election. And each State normal school shall be entitled to twenty scholarships in addition to the scholarships it may have by reason of such town scholarships.

R. L. sec. 467, amended by 1892, No. 24, sec. 1.

SEC. 34. The town superintendent may appoint to a scholarship, for the period required to complete a course of study in the school, any person who is an inhabitant of the town, of good character, fifteen years of age or more, who declares it to be his purpose to complete at least one of the courses of study in the normal school, and to teach in the common schools of the State for two years after graduation; and upon passing the examination for admission to the school, such person shall be entitled to the privileges thereof. The town superintendent shall notify the trustees of the school of such appointment before the first day of the term in which the appointment is to take effect.

R. L. sec. 468, amended by 1888, No. 9, sec. 292, and 1890, No. 5, sec. 1.

SEC. 35. If the scholarship of the town is already filled through appointment by himself or by his predecessor, he may recommend for scholarship to the trustees of either of the normal schools, any person whom he could appoint to the scholarship of his town.

R. L. sec. 469, amended by 1888, No. 9, sec. 292, and 1890, No. 5, sec. 1.

SEC. 36. A scholarship vacant by the failure of the town superintendent to appoint a suitable person, or by the unexcused absence of the holder of the scholarship, may be assigned, by the trustees, for one term only, to any person recommended by a town superintendent and who passes the required examination. But no town shall have more than ten scholarships in one term.

R. L. 470, amended by 1888, No. 9, sec. 292, 1890, No. 5, sec. 1, and 1892,
No. 24, sec. 1.

SEC. 37. A scholarship shall be reckoned at twelve dollars a half year; and the trustees of each normal school may present their claim to the auditor of accounts in the months of June and December for such sum as will be produced by the number of scholarships filled in their school for the half year then current. The State superintendent, during each half year, shall examine the records of each normal school, and if he finds that the scholarships have been granted according to law and only in such numbers as the law allows, and that the provisions of law respecting courses of study have been complied with, shall give his certificate to that effect; and the auditor shall draw his order on the treasurer of the State for the amount of the claim presented by the trustees only when the claim is accompanied by such a certificate from the State superintendent.

R. L. sec. 471.

SEC. 38. Five hundred dollars a year is appropriated to each normal school, to be expended by the trustees thereof under the direction of the State superintendent, in aiding such schools ; and the auditor of accounts shall draw his order on the treasurer of the State, for one-half of the above named sum in each of the months of June and December, on the presentation by the trustees of such school of their claim therefor, with a certificate of the State superintendent that the school has complied with the provisions of law respecting normal schools.

R. L. sec. 472.

SEC. 39. The additional sum of one thousand five hundred dollars a year is hereby appropriated to each of the normal schools in the State, to be expended by the trustees thereof, under the direction of the State superintendent, in aiding such school; and the auditor of accounts shall draw his order on the treasurer of the State, in the month of December, on the presentation by the trustees of such school of their claim therefor, with a certificate of the State superintendent that the school has complied with the law respecting normal schools.

1882, No. 27, sec. 1, and 1892, No. 23, sec. 1.

SEC. 40. If, in addition to all sums received from the State by direct appropriation, from State scholarships, from tuition and from the rent of county grammar school lands, the trustees of a normal school shall, in any year, furnish and use, under the direction of the State superintendent, for the current expenses of the school, the sum of five hundred dollars, they shall receive from the State an equal sum which shall be used in paying for instruction in such school. The auditor of accounts shall draw his order for the payment of such sum in half yearly installments, in June and December, upon the receipt of the claim of the trustees therefor accompanied by a certificate from the State superintendent that the condition upon which such sum is appropriated has been complied with.

R. L. sec. 473.

Sec. 41. A graded school organized in accordance with a special act of the General Assembly, and situated in a county in which there is no normal school, may establish, in connection with such graded school, a training school department for the instruction and training of teachers. The State superintendent shall establish two courses of study in such training school similar to those of normal schools. The examining board for such training school shall be composed of the State superintendent, the principal of the school and the examiner appointed for the normal school in the same congressional district. Such board shall have the same powers and be liable to the same duties as the examining board of a normal school.

R. L. sec. 474.

CHAPTER IV.

TEACHERS' CERTIFICATES.

SECTION 42. No person shall teach a public school without having a certificate or a permit as hereinafter provided, and a contract for teaching shall be void if the teacher does not obtain said certificate or permit before opening school; but this provision shall not apply to the principal teacher of the highest department of a graded school. No certificate shall be granted to a person not seventeen years of age.

1888, No. 9, sec. 40, amended by 1890, No. 5, sec. 4.

SEC. 43. A certificate of graduation from the lower course of a normal school in this State, shall be a license to teach in the public schools of the State for five years from the date thereof; and a certificate of graduation from the higher course of such normal school shall be a license to teach in the public schools of the State for ten years from the date thereof.

1888, No. 9, sec. 41.

SEC. 44. A graduate from the lower course of the normal school, at the fifth annual examination after his graduation, on presenting to the examining board of such school satisfactory evidence that he has taught successfully in the public schools of the State one hundred weeks since his graduation, may be admitted to an examination in the higher course of study in said school, and on passing a satisfactory examination therein, shall receive a certificate thereof from the board of trustees of said school, which shall be a license to teach for ten years in the public schools of the State.

1888, No. 9, sec. 42.

SEC. 45. A graduate of such normal school holding a ten years' certificate, who has taught two hundred weeks under such certificate, may, at the expiration thereof, be granted by the concurrent action of the superintendent of education and the examiner of schools of the county where such person last taught, without examination, a certificate authorizing such person to teach in the public schools of the State until such certificate is revoked by like concurrent action.

1888, No. 9, sec. 43, amended by 1890, No. 5, sec. 2.

SEC. 46. An examiner of schools may grant to graduates from the highest course of a normal school in another state, certificates of qualification, which shall in his own county confer the same authority to teach, and be subject to the same provisions, as certificates of graduation from the same course of a normal school of this State.

1888, No. 9, sec. 44, amended by 1890, No, 5, sec. 2.

SEC. 47. The superintendent of education shall· prepare printed questions for examinations and blanks for teachers' certificates, and shall transmit the same to the examiners; he shall also fix the standard which shall be reached in the examinations.

1890, No. 5, sec. 12.

SEC. 48. All examination papers shall be preserved at the office of the examiner, at least one year, and be subject to the inspection of the superintendent of education. No person shall be employed or paid for services as teacher unless he shall exhibit to the prudential committee [or school directors] a State certificate from the examiner, or a permit from the town superintendent, that he is qualified to teach the school for which he may apply.

1890, No. 5, sec. 13.
See secs. 43 and 44.

SEC. 49. The (said) examiner, after consultation with the town superintendents of the county, shall, in the spring and autumn of each year, make arrangements for a public examination of applicants for teachers' certificates, at such places and times as shall best accommodate the teachers of the county, at as many places as may be agreed upon by the examiner and superintendents; and candidates for examination may choose which of said examinations they will attend.

1890, No. 5, sec. 3.

SEC. 50. Such examination shall be both oral and written, and shall be conducted by the examiner, but if he be prevented by sickness or other cause, he may employ some competent person to conduct such examination; and the examiner may afterward grant certificates, upon the examination papers and the report of the person who conducted the examination; and should such examiner be unable to issue seasonable certificates, then the State superintendent shall issue such certificates, and said certificates shall be of the same validity as if issued by the examiner.

1890, No. 5, sec. 3.

SEC. 51. The examiner shall issue certificates of three grades, viz: A certificate of the first grade shall be given only to one who has taught forty weeks successfully, and whose examination papers shall have shown the applicant to have reached the standard required by the State superintendent, shall have passed a satisfactory oral examination, and shall have given evidence of good moral character and ability to govern; such certificate shall be a license to teach for five years from its date, in any town in the State. A certificate of the second grade shall be granted only to one who has taught successfully twelve weeks, and shall have passed a satisfactory examination in all branches required by law to be taught in common schools, and whose examination papers shall have shown the applicant to have reached the standard required by the State superintendent of education, and shall have given evidence of good moral character and ability to govern; such certificate shall be a license to teach for two years from its date, in any town in the State. A certificate of the third grade shall be a license to teach for a specified time, not to exceed one year, and may, at the discretion of the examiner, be limited to the teaching of a particular school. A person who has twice taken a certificate of the third grade, and who has taught at least twenty-four weeks, shall not afterwards be given a certificate of that grade.

1890, No. 5, sec. 5.

SEC. 52. Said examiner may also give an applicant a private examination, when in his judgment the exigencies of the case may require the same. Said examiner shall furnish to each person examined by him a certified statement of the percentage attained by such person in the different branches in which he has been examined at any given examination, and shall keep a record of the name, age and residence of each person examined by him, and the date and grade of each certificate issued; no applicant who shall fail to pass the required examination shall have another examination within three months thereafter; and should any person obtain a certificate contrary to the provisions of this act, such certificate shall be void.

1890, No. 5, sec. 6.

SEC. 53. Certificates held by teachers employed continuously in graded and union schools, shall remain in force for such length of time as the holders of such certificates continue in the employ of such graded or union school.

1890, No. 5, sec. 7.

SEC. 54. A school maintained by a town or district not less than thirty weeks each year, and consisting of three or more departments, taught by four or more teachers, having an established course of study, and having all the departments under control of one principal teacher, shall be a graded school.

1888, No. 9, sec. 102.

SEC. 55. A graduate of any college whose course of study is approved by the superintendent of education, who has taught in the public schools of the State twenty-four weeks, may receive from the supervisor [examiner] of schools of the county where such person last taught, without examination, a ertificate of the first grade, if in the judgment of the supervisor [examiner], such person has fully proved his ability to instruct and govern.

1888, No. 9, sec. 57.

SEC. 56. A person who has held examiners' certificates of the first grade for ten successive years, and has during that time taught two hundred weeks in the public schools of the State, may, at the end of such time, be granted the certificate provided for in section forty-three [section forty-five of this compilation] in the same manner and with the same effect.

1888, No. 9, sec. 59, amended by 1890, No. 5. sec. 2.

SEC. 57. A teacher holding a State certificate shall notify the town superintendent of the county [town] in which he is to teach before commencing his school that he holds such certificate, and shall submit the same to the inspection of the town superintendent on request.

1888, No. 9, sec. 60, amended by 1890, No. 5, sec. 2.

SEC. 58. The town superintendent may issue permits to teachers to teach particular schools for a single term ; but such permits shall not be renewed more than three times to any one person, nor shall more than three such permits be granted in one town during the same school term.

1890, No. 5, sec. 14.

SEC. 59. The superintendent of education shall procure the printing of the questions prepared for written examinations, and the cost of such printing shall be allowed as a part of his expenses. The advertising and other necessary expenses of a public examination of teachers shall be paid by the supervisor [examiner] and be repaid him upon the settlement of his account.

1888, No. 9, sec. 65.

CHAPTER V.

MAINTENANCE OF SCHOOLS.—TOWN SYSTEM.

SECTION 60. After the date on which this act shall take effect, [April 1st, 1893], each town in this State shall constitute a single district for school purposes, and the divisions of the town into school districts heretofore existing, shall no longer exist, except for the settlement of their pecuniary affairs.

But school districts organized under special acts of the Legislature, and school districts in unorganized towns and gores shall in no way be affected by the provisions of this act, unless, at a meeting legally warned, they shall vote to become part of the town district system.

1892, No. 20, sec. 1.

SEC. 61. In towns having a graded school district chartered by a special act of the Legislature, the voters in said graded school district shall not be entitled to vote in town meetings in any matters pertaining to the schools of the town district, or for the election of school officers in such town.

1892, No. 21, sec. 23.

SEC. 62. The several towns shall take charge of the school houses and property belonging thereto, within their respective limits, and all debts outstanding that have accrued for the purchase of land, erection of school houses and repairs on school houses, shall be audited and paid by the respective towns. All other indebtedness of any school district shall be paid by said district in the settlement of their pecuniary affairs.

1892, No. 20, sec. 2.

SEC. 63. The selectmen shall, during the year 1893, appraise the school houses and the property belonging thereto in the school districts of their town, which appraisal, together with the district's indebtedness assumed by the town under the town system act, shall be recorded in the town clerk's office in their respective towns.

1892, No. 21, sec. 20.

SEC. 64. Such town shall provide and maintain suitable school houses, and the location, construction and sale of the same shall be under the control of the board of school directors.

1888, No. 9, sec. 138.

SEC. 65. In case of fractional districts, parts of which belong to different towns, the selectmen of such towns shall appraise and adjust such school property of such fractional districts, abolished under the provisions of this act, and shall make an equitable apportionment of the property and debts of such district, and find the balance equitably due from either of said towns to any of said towns and order such balance to be paid within a time to be by them limited.

1892, No. 20, sec. 3.

SEC. 66. In case of fractional districts between different towns or counties, said appraisal and indebtedness assumed by the towns shall be made and ascertained by the selectmen of the respective towns concerned in such fractional districts, and an apportionment of such indebtedness shall be made to the towns interested therein, by such selectmen, which appraisal and apportionment shall be recorded in the town clerk's office of each interested town; but if such selectmen cannot agree, the State superintendent of education shall determine and establish such fractional district appraisal and apportionment.

1892, No. 21, sec. 21.

SEC. 67. At the annual town meeting in March, 1893, there shall be elected a board of three or six school directors, citizens of the town, one-third of whom shall be elected for one year, one-third for two years and one third for three years, and at every annual town meeting thereafter, one-third of whom shall be elected for three years. A vacancy in the board shall be filled by appointment by the selectmen, until the next annual town meeting, when the town shall elect a director for the remainder of the unexpired term.

All directors elected or appointed shall hold office until their successors are elected.

1892, No. 20, sec. 4.

SEC. 67 a. The school directors shall be sworn, and shall, on or before the first day of April in each year, elect one of their number chairman, and appoint some person, not one of their number, to be clerk of the board.

1888, No. 9, sec. 127, amended by 1890, No. 5 sec. 2. See sec. 78.

SEC. 68. The school officers provided for by law shall be voted for upon a separate ballot, which shall be deposited in a ballot box other than that in which other ballots are deposited, and women shall have the same right that men have to vote on all matters pertaining to schools and school officers in towns, cities and graded school districts; and the same right to hold offices relating to school affairs, except in cases where it may be otherwise provided.

1888, No. 9, sec. 92, amended by 1892, No. 21, sec. 22.

SEC. 69. Said board of school directors shall have the care of the school property of the town and the management of its schools, determine the number and location of its schools, employ teachers and fix their compensation, examine and allow claims arising in school matters and draw orders upon the town treasurer for the payment thereof, and shall, in general, have the powers and perform all the duties heretofore devolving upon the prudential committee and clerk of a school district; and may make regulations not inconsistent with the law, for carrying the powers granted them into effect.

1892, No. 20, sec. 5.

SEC. 70. School districts [directors] shall have power to purchase sites, erect school houses, or sell buildings or sites, when authorized by a vote of their respective towns so to do.

1892, No. 21, sec. 19.

SEC. 71. In every town there shall be kept for at least twenty-six weeks in each year, at the expense of said town, by a teacher or teachers of competent ability and of good morals, a sufficient number of schools for the instruction of all the children who may legally attend all the public schools therein; and all pupils shall be thoroughly instructed in good behavior, reading, writing, spelling, English grammar, geography, arithmetic, free hand drawing, the history and constitution of the United States and in elementary physiology and hygiene, and shall receive special instruction in the geography, history, constitution and principles of the government of Vermont. Said school shall be within the limits of said town, and at such places, and held at such times as in the judgment of the board of directors will best subserve the interests of education and give all the scholars of the town as nearly equal advantages as may be practicable; and said school board may use a portion of the school money, not exceeding twenty-five per cent thereof, for the purpose of conveying scholars to and from such schools.

1892, No. 20, sec. 6.

SEC. 72. The board of school directors may provide for the instruction of advanced pupils in the higher branches of English study in one or more of the graded schools of the town, and may establish central schools in said town.

1892, No. 20, sec. 7.

SEC. 73. The board of school directors may receive into the schools under their charge pupils residing in other towns, in the same manner and under the same restrictions, as provided in the case of school districts; and moneys received for the instruction of non-resident pupils shall be paid into the school fund of the town.

1892, No. 20, sec. 8.

SEC. 74. Said board may provide for the instruction of any legal pupils of the town in the public schools of an adjoining town, and may pay for such instruction from the school moneys of the town.

1892, No. 20, sec. 9.

SEC. 75. Towns may, by vote, authorize the directors to provide for the education of advanced pupils of school age in any graded or incorporated school or academy within the limits of the town.

1892, No. 21, sec. 24.

SEC. 76. The board of school directors shall, at each annual town meeting, present to the town a full report of their doings, with an exhibit of orders drawn by them for the use of schools.

1892, No. 20, sec. 10.

SEC. 77. The compensation of school directors shall be such sum as may be voted by the towns at their annual March meeting for time actually spent in the performance of their duties, and the same shall be paid out of the town treasury; but their account shall be audited and allowed like that of other town officers.

1892, No. 20, sec. 11.

SEC. 78. The said directors shall also appoint a clerk of the board; said clerk shall keep a permanent record book and record therein the proceedings of the board; and he shall make the registration returns to town clerks required to be made, and take the school census required to be taken by school district clerks, and he shall receive the same compensation therefor.

1892, No. 20, sec. 13.

CHAPTER VI.

SCHOOL AGE.—ATTENDANCE.

SECTION 79. The term "legal pupils" shall include all persons between the ages of five and twenty-one years. No child under five years of age shall be received as a pupil into any of the public schools of the State. But school directors may establish a kindergarten school for the instruction of the children of the town under five years of age.

1892, No. 21, sec. 1.

3

SEC. 80. The term "school age" shall include persons between the ages of five and twenty-one years.

1892, No. 22, sec. 1.

SEC. 81. The selectmen of each town and the mayor of each city shall annually appoint two truant officers for their respective towns and cities. On failure to appoint such truant officers, constables, sheriffs, deputy sheriffs and policemen, shall act as truant officers.

1892, No. 22. sec. 2.

SEC. 82. Every person having under his control a child of good health and sound mind between eight and fourteen years of age, shall cause such child to attend a public school at least twenty weeks in the year, unless such child has been otherwise furnished with the means of education for a like period of time, or has already acquired the branches of study required by law to be taught in the common schools.

1892, No. 22, sec. 3.

SEC. 83. No child under fourteen years of age, shall be employed in a mill or factory unless such child shall have attended a public school twenty weeks during the preceding year, and shall deposit with the owner or person in charge of such mill or factory a certificate showing such attendance, signed by the teacher of such school.

1892, No. 22, sec. 4.

SEC. 84. The town superintendent of schools may inquire of the owner or person in charge of a mill or factory as to the employment of children therein; and may call for the production of the certificates required to be deposited with such person, and ascertain if there is any violation of the law in the employment of such children.

1892, No. 22, sec. 5.

SEC. 85. No person shall hereafter give employment to any child under fourteen years of age who cannot read and write, but is capable of receiving such instruction, during the time when the school which such person should attend is in session.

1892, No. 22, sec. 6.

SEC. 86. A person who shall violate the provisions of sections three, four, or six of this act, [sections eighty-two, eighty-three and eighty-five of this compilation], or who shall refuse to give the information or exhibit the certificates required to be given and exhibited by section five of this act, [section eighty-four of this compilation], shall forfeit not less than five nor more than twenty-five dollars, to be recovered by prosecution before a justice of the peace and to be paid to the town in which the child resides. And each truant officer is hereby required to make complaint of any violation of said sections to a justice of the peace or judge of a municipal court, who shall issue his warrant, according to law, for the arrest and trial of such offender.

1892, No. 22, sec. 7.

SEC. 87. Each teacher shall promptly give notice to the school director of each violation of section three of this act, [section eighty-two of this compilation], by any pupil enrolled in his school, and the director shall immediately notify a truant officer of such violation. The truant officer shall forthwith inquire into the cause of the pupil's non-attendance, and if he has reason to believe that such pupil's parent, guardian or master has violated said section the truant officer shall immediately make complaint to a justice of the peace or judge of the municipal court, and such justice or court shall issue a warrant directed to any sheriff or constable in the State commanding him forthwith to arrest and bring before said justice or court such parent, guardian or master and such child; and upon proof that said parent, guardian or master is guilty of violating said section he shall be fined by said justice or court not less than five nor more than twenty-five dollars, which shall be paid into the treasury of the town.

1892, No. 22, sec. 8.

SEC. 88. If on trial, it shall appear that the child is not clothed properly for attending school, and that his parent is unable to so clothe him, the overseer of the poor shall furnish suitable clothes for the child; and such inability of the parent shall be a defence to a prosecution under this act. But if it appears that the parent in unable to control the said child and keep him in school, the justice or court with the consent of the majority of the selectmen, may sentence him to the reform school in accordance with the provisions of law when persons between eight and fourteen years have committed crime.

1892, No. 22, sec. 9.

SEC. 89. The truant officer of a town, or a member of the board of school directors, or any officer authorized to make arrests in the town may arrest, and upon the written application of three voters in the town shall arrest, a child who, under the provisions of section three of this act, [section eighty-two of this compilation], is required to attend school, and who, during a term of the public school in the town in which he resides, is habitually found in the streets or other public places, having no lawful occupation, or who is an habitual truant; and shall take him to the school in said town and place him in charge of the teacher thereof; and shall give notice thereof in writing to the parent, guardian or master therein requiring him to cause such child to attend school regularly.

1892, No. 22, sec. 10.

SEC. 90. If such parent, guardian or master does not cause such child to attend school regularly after receiving such notice, for the remainder of the term of school for which such arrest was made, having no good reason for failure so to do, the officer making the arrest shall make complaint to a justice of the peace or judge of the municipal court, and such justice or judge shall issue a warrant directed to any sheriff or constable in the State, commanding him forthwith to arrest and bring before said justice or court such parent, guardian or master, and such child; and upon proof that the child was liable to arrest, as provided in the preceding section, and that the parent, guardian or master has received and not complied with the notice and requirement before specified, the justice or court shall fine such parent, guardian or master not less than five nor more than twenty-five dollars, to be paid into the treasury of the town.

1892, No. 22, sec. 11.

SEC. 91. The complaint shall be sufficient if it states that said parent, master or guardian neglects to send to school as required by law, his child, apprentice or ward, naming such child, apprentice or ward; and prosecutions under such complaint shall be conducted like criminal prosecutions, and an appeal may in like manner be had to the county court.

1892, No. 22, sec. 12.

SEC. 92. The truant officer of a town or a school director, or officer authorized to make arrests in the town, who shall refuse or neglect to carry out the provisions of sections three, seven, eight and eleven of this act, [sections eighty-two eighty-six, eighty-seven and ninety of this compilation], shall be fined not exceeding one hundred dollars. A justice of the peace or judge of the municipal court shall have concurrent jurisdiction with the county court in such prosecution.

1892, No. 22, sec. 13.

SEC. 93. All persons acting as truant officers shall receive compensation at the rate of two dollars per day for time actually spent, unless otherwise provided for.

1892, No. 22, sec. 15.

CHAPTER VII.

SCHOOL YEAR.—CENSUS.

SECTION 94. The school year shall commence on the first day of April and end on the last day of March following. In the absence of express contract, a session of three hours in the forenoon and three in the afternoon shall constitute a school day, five such days a school week, and four such weeks a school month.

1892, No. 21, sec. 2.

SEC. 95. Each district shall maintain a school at least twenty-four weeks [in schools under the town system, twenty-six weeks] in the school year. No school shall be taught between the last day of June and the last Monday in August, without the written permission of the town superintendent of schools.

1888, No. 9, sec. 164, amended by 1890, No. 5, sec. 2; also see sec. 71, ante.

SEC. 96. The time, not exceeding four days, actually spent by the teacher of a common school in attendance upon a teachers' institute or State teachers' association, during the time for which such teacher is engaged to teach, shall, in determining the compensation of the teacher, and the number of weeks taught by such teacher, be accounted the same as if spent in teaching.

1892, No. 21, sec. 3.

SEC. 97. A public school teacher shall not be required to teach or perform other service on any day made a legal holiday by the laws of this State, and no deduction shall be made from his time or compensation because of his absence on such days; and such days shall not be deducted in determining the number of weeks of school taught by said teacher.

1892, No. 21, sec. 4.

SEC. 98. The clerk of the board of school directors shall annually, on or before the 20th day of March, prepare an accurate list, containing the name and age of each child of school age residing in the town district, and the name of the parent or other person having control of such child; and he shall keep such list on file, and make such report therefrom as the superintendent of education may require.

1892, No. 21. sec. 5.

SEC. 99. If a parent or other person having control of a child between the ages of five and twenty-one years shall refuse to give the clerk information as to the age of such child, or shall falsely state the same, he shall be fined not more than twenty nor less than five dollars.

1892, No. 21, sec. 6.

SEC. 100. A clerk of the board of school directors shall receive from the treasury of the town, and a clerk of a graded school district from the treasurer of said district, for taking such census, a sum equal to four cents for each person of school age in the district.

1892, No. 21, sec. 7.

CHAPTER VIII.

REGISTERS AND RETURNS.

SECTION 101. The superintendent of education shall prescribe blank forms for a school register for keeping a record of the daily attendance of pupils, and interrogatories to be printed in said register for procuring the statistical information required to be given by teachers, town and graded school officers, and for procuring such further information as he may think desirable.

1892, No. 21, sec. 8.

SEC. 102. The superintendent of education shall annually, in the month of February, transmit to town clerks a sufficient number of such registers to supply the schools in their respective towns ; and a town clerk receiving such registers shall immediately forward to the superintendent a receipt therefor.

1892, No. 21, sec. 9.

SEC. 103. The clerk of the board of school directors shall annually, on or before the 20th day of March, procure from the town clerk a register for each school in his town, and shall be responsible for the safekeeping thereof.

1892, No. 21, sec. 10.

SEC. 104. A teacher shall before commencing school procure a register from the clerk of the board of directors, and shall keep therein, in the prescribed form, a record of the daily attendance of each pupil, and shall enter therein correct answers to the interrogatories addressed to teachers, and shall return such register to the clerk of the board of directors, at the end of each term, the final return to be on or before the 20th day of March.

1892, No. 21, sec. 11.

SEC. 105. Upon the return of such register said clerk shall examine the same, and if he finds it filled out as required by law, and properly certified to by the teacher, he shall give such teacher a certificate to that effect; and the teacher shall not be entitled to his compensation except on presentation of the certificate of said clerk to the chairman of the board of directors, who shall draw an order on the town treasurer for the payment of said teacher.

1892, No. 21, sec. 12.

SEC. 106. The said clerk, upon the final return to him of the register, shall enter therein correct answers to the interrogatories to be answered by the clerk, and the chairman of the board of directors shall enter therein the name of the teacher of the school during the year for which such register was kept, and the date and character of such teacher's certificate, and certify to the correctness of such entry, and said clerk shall file each register so completed in the office of the town clerk before the last Friday preceding the last Tuesday in March.

1892, No. 21, sec. 13.

SEC. 107. The duties to be performed by clerks of boards of directors, as provided by sections 10, 12 and 13, [sections 103, 105 and 106], shall apply to clerks of graded school districts, chartered by special acts of the legislature; and the duties of teachers required in section 11 [section 104] shall apply to teachers of said graded school.

1892, No. 21, sec. 14.

SEC. 108. The town clerk shall annually, in the month of April, or at such time as the State superintendent of education may direct, make out and return to said State superintendent such statistics as he may require, said State superintendent to prepare and furnish suitable blanks therefor. Upon the receipt of such statistics the State superintendent of education shall return to said town clerk a certificate of such receipt.

1892, No. 21, sec. 15.

SEC. 109. Trustees of incorporated academies and grammar schools shall cause their principals to return to the superintendent of education, on or before the first day of April annually, answers to the statistical inquiries addressed to them by said superintendent.

1892, No. 21, sec. 16.

SEC. 110. For all services rendered as required by this act, the town clerk shall receive from the town treasury a sum equal to three cents for each person of school age in the town, but such compensation shall not be less than three nor more than twenty dollars.

1892, No. 21, sec. 17.

CHAPTER IX.

SCHOOL TAXES AND SCHOOL MONEYS.

I. SCHOOL TAXES.

SECTION 111. The grand list of the town district shall be made up of the ratable polls, the real estate and personal property taxable therein.

1892, No. 21, sec. 18.

SEC. 112. The school directors of each town shall annually in writing recommend to the selectmen of said town the amount of money necessary for the use of schools, and said selectmen shall annually appropriate for such purpose a sum not exceeding one-half, nor less than one-fifth, of the grand list of such town, and shall assess a tax annually to defray such appropriations. Any town by special vote may raise a larger sum for school purposes.

1892, No. 20, sec. 14.

Sec. 113. The treasurer of such town shall keep a separate account of the moneys appropriated or given for the use of schools, and shall pay out of such moneys orders drawn by the board of school directors for the use of schools.

1892, No. 20, sec. 15.

II. United States Deposit Money.

Sec. 114. The treasurer of the State shall receive moneys belonging to the United States to be deposited with this State and give a certificate of deposit for the same according to law.

1888, No. 9, sec. 210.

Sec. 115. Such moneys shall be apportioned to the several towns, organized and unorganized, and to the gores, in proportion to the number of inhabitants in each. When a census is taken under the laws of Congress or of this State, a new apportionment shall be made. If upon such new apportionment it appears that a town has more than its share, the treasurer of the State shall demand and recover from such town such excess; and if a town has less than its share, he shall make up the deficiency to such town.

1888, No. 9, sec. 211.

Sec. 116. The treasurer of the State shall pay over to the trustees of the public money in each town which has elected such trustees, provided such trustees have executed the required bond, the share of the deposit money apportioned to such town.

1888, No. 9, sec. 212.

Sec. 117. Such trustees shall receive such town's share of the deposit money, and shall give the treasurer of the State a receipt therefor, similar to that given by said treasurer to the secretary of the treasury of the United States; and said trustees shall manage such money and report the condition of the same at each annual town meeting.

1888, No. 9, sec. 213.

Sec. 118. Such trustees, before entering upon the duties of their office, shall execute a bond to the town, with at least three sufficient sureties in such sum as the selectmen direct, conditioned to the faithful performance of their duties in loaning, managing, accounting for and paying over, as may be required by law, the moneys placed in their charge under the provisions of this chapter. And if a trustee fails to execute such bond his office shall be vacant and such vacancy may be filled as in other cases of vacancies in town offices.

1888, No. 9, sec. 214.

Sec. 119. The trustees of the public money may loan the same to the town, if the town at a meeting warned for that purpose authorizes the selectmen to borrow it. If the money is not loaned to the town, the trustees shall loan the same with sufficient personal security, or on mortgage, as they may deem safe, made payable to the respective towns at an interest of six per cent annually. Such loans shall be made for a term not exceeding one year; and the moneys may be collected at the expiration of the term and loaned to other persons, or the loan may be extended to the same persons for an additional period. The trustees shall annually, previous to the first day of March, pay to the town treasurer the income received from such moneys.

1888, No. 9, sec. 215, amended by 1890, No. 5, sec. 2.

SEC. 120. The treasurer of the State shall retain the share apportioned to towns which have not elected trustees, and the shares of unorganized towns and gores, and shall annually, previous to the first day of June, pay to the treasurer of each organized town not electing trustees, and to the treasurers of school districts in unorganized towns and gores which have maintained schools for the required length of time during the previous year, the interest upon the shares apportioned to such towns and gores. And he shall divide the interest money of each unorganized town or gore among the school districts therein in the manner provided for the distribution of town school moneys among the several districts in towns.

1888, No. 9, sec. 216.

SEC. 121. The treasurer of each town shall give credit in his account of the school fund, for all sums received by him as income from the town share of the deposit money.

1888, No. 9, sec. 217.

SEC. 122. The income from the deposit money received by each town shall be annually appropriated to the support of schools in the town. But if a town has other school funds, the income of which is sufficient to support schools in all the districts in such town for six months in each year, such town may appropriate the income received from its share of such money to the support of schools or to any purpose.

1888, No. 9, sec. 218.

SEC. 123. Towns which have received their portion of the deposit money shall be accountable for the same, or any part thereof, when required by the treasurer of the State on requisition of the United States, or for the purpose of a new apportionment, as towns are accountable for State taxes.

1888, No. 9, sec. 219.

SEC. 124. If a town fails to comply with the provisions of this chapter, relative to the management or disposition of the United States moneys, received by such town, it shall forfeit to the treasurer of the county, for the use of such county, a sum not exceeding double the amount of the interest on such moneys.

1888, No. 9, sec. 220.

Sec. 125. The grand jury shall inquire how the towns have managed and disposed of the moneys so deposited with them, and the annual interest thereof; and if a town has not complied with the provisions of this chapter, relative to such deposit money, they shall present to the court their indictment therefor against the town; and notice thereof shall be given to such town as is required in case of indictment for not repairing highways.

1888, No. 9, sec. 221.

Sec. 126. The treasurer of the State, in the collection of the United States deposit money loaned by former treasurers, shall adjust and settle the same as is for the interest of the State.

1888, No. 9, sec. 222.

III. Town School Fund.

Sec. 127. The selectmen of a town shall have charge of the real and personal estate in such town appropriated as a fund to the use of schools therein, unless otherwise provided for by law, or unless the person giving any part thereof directs the same to be managed in some other way, and shall annually render an account to the town of their proceedings in connection therewith; and the selectmen shall lease lands appropriated for such purpose, and loan moneys on annual or semi-annual interest, with sufficient security, and for such security may take mortgages or deeds of any real estate in the State.

1888, No. 9. sec. 223.

Sec. 128. The securities for the payment of the moneys so loaned and the interest thereon, shall be taken in the name of the town, and the selectmen may, in the name of the town, prosecute and defend actions for the recovery or protection of the estate so intrusted to their care; and if the title or possession of real estate mortgaged or deeded as security is recovered in such action, the selectmen may, in the name of the town, lease or sell and convey such real estate, and invest the moneys received therefrom as provided in the preceding section.

1888, No. 9, sec. 224.

Sec. 129. A person authorized to take the acknowledgment of deeds may take the acknowledgment of a deed provided for in the two preceding sections, or may sign such deed as witness, although he is an inhabitant and tax-payer of the town.

1888, No. 9, sec. 225.

Sec. 130. The securities belonging to the town school fund shall be deposited in the office of the treasurer of the town; and moneys received on account of the same, shall be paid into such treasury; and a separate account of the same shall be kept on the books of the treasurer.

1888, No. 9, sec. 226.

IV. STATE SCHOOL TAX.

Sec. 131. A tax of five cents on the dollar shall be annually assessed on the list of the polls and ratable estate of the inhabitants of this State for the support of the common schools.

1890, No. 6, sec. 1.

Sec. 132. The treasurer of the State shall apportion to the several towns and cities and unorganized towns and gores in this State such tax according to their respective lists, and shall on or before the first day of May, in each year, make out and transmit to the treasurer of each town and city and to the collector of taxes for the unorganized towns and gores in this State, a notice of the amount so apportioned and that the same shall be paid into the treasury of the State on or before the first day of June next following.

1890, No. 6, sec. 2.

Sec. 133. The commissioners of taxes for all unorganized towns and gores shall immediately upon receipt of such notice assess a tax for the amount specified and cause the same to be collected in the manner prescribed by law upon such unorganized towns and gores, and cause the same to be paid into the State treasury according to such notice; and the several town and city treasurers shall, upon the receipt of such notice, transmit the same to the selectmen or mayor of their respective towns or cities, and such selectmen or mayor shall draw an order on the treasurer of their respective town or city for the amount of such tax and such treasurer shall pay the same to the State treasurer according to such notice, out of any moneys belonging to their town or city, and if there is not sufficient funds in the hands of such treasurer to pay such tax, the selectmen or mayor shall borrow the same upon their orders and the several towns or cities may provide for the payment of such tax by a special tax to be assessed and collected like ordinary town or city taxes, or such State tax may be provided for like ordinary expenses of the several towns or cities.

1890, No. 6, sec. 3.

Sec. 134. The list prepared annually by the secretary of State from the abstracts of the grand list of the several towns, cities, unorganized towns or gores, which are now by law required to be returned to his office shall constitute a basis for the apportionment of said tax.

1890, No. 6, sec. 4.

SEC. 135. The provisions of section three hundred and sixty-nine of the Revised Laws shall not apply to taxes assessed by this act.

1890, No. 6, sec. 5.

SEC. 136. The treasurer of the State shall annually, on or before the tenth day of July, divide the money in the treasury of the State, received on such tax, among the towns, cities and unorganized towns or gores, in proportion to the number of legal schools sustained the preceding school year, which sum shall, in towns or cities having the town system or [and] graded school district, be divided as now provided by law for the division of school moneys. Such money shall be divided by the selectmen of each town on or before the 15th day of September in each year.

1890, No. 6, sec. 6, amended by 1891, Special Session, No. 2, sec. 1, and 1892, No. 20, sec. 1.

CHAPTER X.

TEXT-BOOKS.

SECTION 137. The county board of education shall, in the year one thousand eight hundred and ninety, and in every fifth year thereafter, select such text-books, one book of a grade in each study; except that in the first selection text-books on physiology and hygiene shall be omitted; and said board shall, in the year one thousand eight hundred and ninety-two, make a selection of text-books so omitted, to have effect until the general selection of text-books three years later.

1888, No. 9, sec. 171.

Sec. 1890, No. 5, sec. 1, also note below.

SEC. 138. The board shall complete a selection of text-books before the first day of April, and within seven days after that date shall publish a report thereof in all the newspapers of the county; and from the first day of

July following until another selection is established the use of any other text-books in the studies prescribed by law in the schools of the county is prohibited. But this shall not be held to prevent the use of such books as may be supplied without expense to the pupils.

1888, No. 9, sec. 172.

SEC. 139. The publisher of any book selected by said board shall be required to enter into a written agreement to furnish for sale in the towns of such county, at such prices as may be therein named for the period of five years, as many of such books as may be required, of the quality and style agreed upon with said board.

1888, No. 9, sec. 173.

SEC. 140. In case of a failure to supply any of the books selected in accordance with the terms of such agreement for the full period required, said board may select other books to be used in their stead until the time of the next regular selection.   '

1888, No. 9, sec. 174.

SEC. 141. The chairman of said board shall arrange with one or more persons in each town to keep for sale the authorized text-books, who shall receive on the sale thereof not more than the freight and express charges and ten per cent advance upon the publishers' contract prices.

1888, No. 9, sec. 175.

SEC. 142. Payment of the expense of publishing the report of the board shall be made by the supervisor, who shall be allowed the same in the settlement of his accounts.

1888, No. 9, sec. 176.

SEC. 143. If a member of the text-book board shall directly or indirectly accept any appointment, gift, private compensation, or promise of reward, for his action in the selection of text-books, he shall be fined not exceeding one thousand dollars and imprisoned not more than one year.

1888, No. 9, sec. 177.

SEC. 144. Text-books on physiology and hygiene shall be furnished pupils in the public schools, at the expense of the State, until July 1, 1895.

1888, No. 9, sec. 178.

SEC. 145. The regulations before prescribed for the supply and return of such books shall continue in force until changed by the county text-book board; and the duties performed by town superintendents under such regulations shall, after the first day of April next [1889], be performed by the town clerks.

1888, No. 9, sec. 179.

SEC. 146. Town clerks shall annually, in the month of April, estimate the number of such books of each kind needed for the school year next ensuing, and forward such estimates to the secretary of State.

1888, No. 9, sec. 180.

SEC. 147. The secretary of State, having received such estimates, shall procure the required books from the contractors and forward the same at the expense of the State to the town clerks; and he shall keep a record of the books ordered, received and distributed, and shall certify to the auditor the amounts due the contractors; and the auditor shall draw orders therefor.

1888, No. 9. sec. 181.

SEC. 148. Such books shall remain the property of the State. Town clerks shall distribute them as the regulations prescribe, and reclaim them when required by such regulations.

1888, No. 9, sec. 182.

SEC. 149. When a pupil is not provided with the required text-books, other than those furnished by the State, the teacher shall notify the prudential committee, [or school directors], and such committee [or directors] shall thereupon give notice of such deficiency to the parent, master or guardian of such pupil ; and if the person notified fails to supply such pupil within one week, the prudential committee [or directors] shall supply him.

1888, No. 9, sec. 183.

See sec. 69, ante, for school directors' authority.

SEC. 150. The prudential committee [or school directors] shall give written notice to the selectmen of the name of each pupil supplied by him, [or them], the name of his parent, master or guardian, and the cost of the books supplied ; and shall receive from the selectmen an order on the town treasurer for the money so expended.

1888, No. 9, sec. 184.

SEC. 151. The selectmen shall, in assessing the next annual tax, add the sum so expended for any pupil to the tax of the parent, master or guardian of such pupil, or may omit a part or all of said sum if such person is unable to pay the same. The amount so added shall be collected and paid into the treasury like a town tax.

1888, No. 9, sec. 185.

SEC. 152. Any town or district may purchase and hold text-books for use in its schools, if it so votes in a meeting warned for that purpose.

1888, No. 9, sec. 186.

SEC. 153. If the superintendent of education or a town superintendent of schools, member of a text-book board, or any teacher in a public school, or other person officially connected with the direction of any public school, shall directly or indirectly receive any gratuity or compensation for recommending or procuring the adoption of a school book, or the purchase of any school apparatus, furniture or other school supplies, in any public school of this State, such person shall be fined not less than twenty nor more than one hundred dollars.

1888, No. 9, sec. 187.

[NOTE.—Sections 137, 140, 142 and 143 are rendered inoperative by No. 5 of the acts of 1890, sec. 1, which abolishes the office of county supervisor and county board of education ; and other sections of the chapter are limited in their provisions by the same act. It is thought best, however, to preserve the chapter intact, so that the provisions of the sections and parts of sections still in operation may be better understood.]

CHAPTER XI.

MISCELLANEOUS PROVISIONS.

SECTION 154. The records of the districts hereby abolished shall be preserved by the town.

1892, No. 20, sec. 16.

SEC. 155. The provisions of all statutes now in force relating to school districts and school officers and their duties, shall be in force so far as the same are consistent with this act; and all acts and parts of acts inconsistent with this act are hereby repealed.

1892, No. 20, sec. 17.

SEC. 156. In towns where the town system has already been adopted the present school directors shall serve until the expiration of their repective term or terms.

1892, No. 21, sec. 32.

SEC. 157. All teachers' certificates in force at the time of the passage of this act [Nov. 26th, 1890,] shall be valid for such time as they were originally issued.

1890, No. 5, sec. 17.

PART II.

Special Provisions Relating to Incorporated School Districts and School Districts in Unorganized Towns and Gores.

CHAPTER XII.

SCHOOL DISTRICTS.

I. ORGANIZATION.

SECTION. 158. The selectmen of a town, on the application of three voters in an adjoining unorganized town or gore, may divide such town or gore into as many school districts as may be needed, and number such districts and organize them in the manner provided in the preceding [following] section. The selectmen acting under this section shall cause their proceedings to be recorded in the office of the clerk of the county in which such town or gore is situated and waive reasonable compensation from the petitioners.

1888, No. 9, sec. 70.

SEC. 158 a. The selectmen shall call a meeting in such district by posting up a notice thereof, specifying the time, place and business of the meeting, in two of the most public places in such district, at least seven days be-

4

fore the time therein specified. One of the selectmen shall preside in the meeting until a moderator and clerk are chosen, when the district shall be held to be organized.

1888, No. 9, sec. 69, amended by 1892, No. 20, sec. 1.

SEC. 159. A school district, legally organized, shall be a body politic and corporate, with the powers of a corporation for maintaining schools in such district, and by its corporate name may sue and be sued, and may take, hold and convey real and personal estate.

1888, No. 9, sec. 71.

II. OFFICERS.

SEC. 160. A school district shall, at its organization, and at each annual meeting thereafter, elect from among the legal voters of such district a moderator, clerk, collector, treasurer, one or three auditors and a prudential committee of one person unless the district shall vote to have the prudential committee of three, provided for in the succeeding section. The term of office of such officers shall commence at the time of their election and continue until their successors are chosen, but if the prudential committee is absent more than three months from the district, his office shall be deemed vacant.

1888, No. 9, sec. 73.

SEC. 161. A school district may, at its organization, or at its annual meeting, elect a prudential committee of three persons, one of whom shall be chosen for one year, one for two years, and one for three years ; and until such district shall vote to discontinue such committee of three such district, shall upon the expiration of the term of office of a member of such committee, elect a successor for three years, and may at any meeting fill a vacancy occurring in said committee.

1888, No. 9, sec. 74.

SEC. 162. If such a committee is elected at the organization of the district, and such organization is not at the time fixed for an annual meeting, the time between the organization and the next annual meeting shall be accounted the first year of said terms.

1888, No. 9, sec. 75.

SEC. 163. When a district has voted to discontinue such committee of three, it shall not elect successors to the members as their terms expire, and the remaining members or member of such committee shall be the committee of the district until the expiration of the term which is last to expire.

1888, No. 9, sec. 76.

SEC. 164. A school district may elect the collector of town taxes, although not an inhabitant of the district, to be collector of such district, if he will accept the office in writing; and such acceptance shall be recorded by the district clerk.

1888, No. 9, sec. 77.

SEC. 165. The moderator shall preside at school district meetings. In case of his absence from a meeting a moderator *pro tempore* may be chosen to preside at such meeting.

1888, No. 9, sec. 78.

SEC. 166. The clerk shall keep a record of the votes and proceedings of school district meetings, and give certified copies thereof when required; and for a willful neglect of such duty he shall forfeit twenty dollars to the district, to be recovered in an action on this statute.

1888, No. 9, sec. 78.

SEC. 167. The clerk shall, within ten days after his election or appointment, give notice thereof, and of the number of his district, to the town clerk; and if he fail to do so he shall receive no compensation for making returns to the town clerk's office.

1888, No. 9, sec. 80.

SEC. 168. The duties of school district collectors, treasurers and auditors, shall be like those of town collectors, town treasurers and town auditors. A district collector or treasurer shall, before entering upon his duties, if required by vote of the district or by the prudential committee, give bonds to the district for the faithful discharge of his duties, in such sum as may be required; and if a collector or treasurer neglects for ten days to give bonds as required, such office shall be vacant.

1888, No. 9, sec. 81.

SEC. 169. The prudential committee shall have the care of the school house and grounds, and shall keep the same in good order, and if there is no school house, shall provide a suitable place for the school; and he shall see that fuel, furniture and all things necessary for the school are provided.

1888, No. 9, sec. 82.

SEC. 170. The prudential committee shall employ a teacher to instruct the school, and may remove him when necessary, and he shall adopt requisite measures, not in conflict with those of the town superintendent of schools, for the inspection, examination, regulation and improvement of the school.

1888, No. 9, sec. 83, amended by 1890, No. 5, sec. 2.

SEC. 171. The prudential committee of a district which has not by vote restricted the action of its committee in the matter, may permit the free use of the school house for religious meetings, lectures, music schools, kindergarten schools and like purposes, when such use will not interfere with the schools or meetings of the district.

1888, No. 9, sec. 84.

Sec. 172. In the absence or disability of the clerk, the prudential committee shall discharge the duties of the clerk, and shall be under the same penalties for a failure therein.

1888, No. 9, sec. 85.

Sec. 173. The prudential committee shall draw orders upon the treasurer for all sums due from the district; but a prudential committee shall not authorize the payment of the moneys of the district to a teacher employed therein who did not obtain a certificate as required by law, or to a teacher whose certificate has been revoked or annulled.

1888, No. 9, sec. 86.

Sec. 174. If a prudential committee shall authorize a payment prohibited in the preceding section, such committee shall be liable to the district for the moneys so paid, to be recovered in an action on this statute; and the town agent shall prosecute such action at the expense and in the name of such district.

1888, No. 9, sec. 87.

Sec. 175. When a vacancy occurs in the office of clerk, collector or treasurer of a school district, or in the office of prudential committee in a district whose committee consists of one person, the selectmen of the town shall fill such vacancy until a new election is made by the appointment of a legal voter of such district, and the district at a special meeting may make a new election.

1888, No. 9, sec. 88.

III. Meetings.

Sec. 176. The annual school meeting shall be held in each district on the last Tuesday in March; and special meetings shall be warned whenever applied for in writing by three voters of the district.

1888, No. 9, sec. 89, amended by 1890, No. 5, sec. 18.

Sec. 177. Nothing in this act shall be so construed as to interfere with the arrangements of any school organized under special acts of the legislature as regards the time for holding their annual meeting.

1890, No. 5. sec. 18.

Sec. 178. School meetings shall be warned by the clerk, or, in case of his absence or neglect, by one of the prudential committee, by posting up, in two of the most public places in the district, at least seven days before the time of the meeting, notices stating the time and place of meeting and the business to be transacted or considered.

1888, No. 9, sec. 90.

SEC. 179.   Persons residing in a school district and qualified to vote in town meeting, shall be voters in school district meetings ; and if a person offering to vote is challenged, the moderator at such meeting, the clerk, and the members of the prudential committee present, shall decide as to his right to vote.

1888, No. 9, sec. 91.

SEC. 180.   The word " meeting " as applied to school district meetings when used in this act, shall mean a school district meeting warned as above provided; and any authority given a district in this act to take any action "by vote," or "by a two-thirds vote," shall mean by vote or by a two-thirds vote, in such a meeting.

1888, No. 9, sec. 93.

SEC. 181.   If a person whose duty it is to warn a school district meeting neglects to do so for ten days after application made as provided by law, he shall forfeit to said district twenty dollars for each ten days' neglect, to be recovered in an action on this statute.

1888, No. 9, sec. 94.

CHAPTER XIII.

MAINTENANCE OF SCHOOLS BY SCHOOL DISTRICTS.

I. SCHOOLS AND INSTRUCTION.

SECTION 182.   All pupils shall be thoroughly instructed in good behavior, reading, writing, spelling, English grammar, geography, arithmetic, free-hand drawing, the history and constitution of the United States, and in elementary physiology and hygiene, giving special prominence to the nature of alcoholic drinks and narcotics, and their effect upon the human system ; and shall receive special instruction in the geography, history, constitution and principles of the government of Vermont.

1888, No. 9, sec. 95.

SEC. 183.   The prudential committee of any district may, if it seems desirable, provide for daily instruction in vocal music by the regular teacher; and any district may, at any regular meeting, instruct its committee to provide for such instruction in vocal music by a teacher employed for that purpose, as it may deem advisable.

1888, No. 9, sec. 96.

SEC. 184.   If the pupils of a district are so numerous as to require more than one teacher, the district may by vote provide for as many schools, or a school of as many departments, as may be needed.

1888, No. 9, sec. 99.

SEC. 185.   In a district having more than one school, or a school of more than one department, the prudential committee may provide for the free instruction of advanced pupils in the higher branches of English study.

1888, No. 9, sec. 100.

SEC. 186.   A district which has made provision for the regular maintenance of schools to be taught by three or more teachers, may by vote direct the teaching of ancient and foreign languages in one or more of such schools.

1888, No. 9, sec. 101.

SEC. 187.   When a district has more than one school, or a school of more than one department, the prudential committee, or a committee chosen by such district for the purpose, shall examine as to the qualifications of the pupils, and designate the school or department which each pupil shall attend.

1888, No. 9, sec. 103.

SEC. 188.   A district maintaining schools taught by twelve or more teachers, may by vote direct its prudential committee to employ a person for the special supervision of such schools; and a person so employed shall, under the general direction of the prudential committee and subject to the control of the town superintendent of schools, superintend the work of the teachers, and perform the duties of the prudential committee in the inspection, examination and regulation of schools.

1888, No. 9, sec. 104, amended by 1890, No. 5, sec. 2.

II. INSTRUCTION PROCURED BY DISTRICT IN OTHER SCHOOLS.

SECTION 189. A district may, under an appropriate article in the warning, by a two-thirds vote, authorize its prudential committee to arrange for the instruction of all its legal pupils, in the studies prescribed by law, in the schools of an adjoining district or districts, or in the most convenient schools of an adjoining town or towns in another state, and may authorize the transportation of such pupils to and from school.

1888, No. 9, sec. 105.

SEC. 190. A prudential committee may, for a reasonable compensation to be paid into the treasury of the district, admit to the school under his charge, the pupils of an adjoining district, by arrangement with the prudential committee of such district.

1888, No. 9, sec. 106.

SEC. 191. If such pupils are provided with not less than twenty-four weeks of instruction within the school year, including such as may have been had in the district of their residence, such district shall be held to have supported a school as required by law, and shall be entitled to its share of the public moneys the same as if a school had been maintained in the district, and the attendance had been in such school.

1888, No. 9, sec. 107.

SEC. 192. A district in a town in which an academy is located may by vote direct its prudential committee to arrange with the officers of such academy for the instruction in such academy of all or a part of the legal pupils of said district in the studies prescribed by law; and if such district continues to maintain a school, it may provide for the instruction of its pupils sent to the academy in the higher branches of English study; and if such district continues to maintain schools taught by three or more teachers, it may provide for the instruction of its pupils sent to the academy in ancient and foreign languages.

1888, No. 9, sec. 108.

SEC. 193. When an arrangement with an academy is such that no school is kept in the district, if all the legal pupils of the district are provided with not less than twenty-four weeks of instruction in the school year, including any that may have been had in the district before the discontinuance of its school, the district shall be held to have supported a school as required by law, and shall be entitled to its share of the public moneys ; and the attendance at an academy of any pupil under an arrangement of the prudential committee as above provided, shall, in the division of public moneys, be treated as an attendance in the school of said district.

1888, No. 9, sec. 109.

SEC. 194. A contract for the instruction of the pupils of a district out of the state or in an academy, shall provide for the keeping and return to the clerk of such district of the attendance of such pupils, in such manner as the keeping and return of attendance is required by law in the school districts of this state; and if such provision of the contract is not complied with, all right to compensation for the instruction of such pupils shall be forfeited.

1888, No. 9, 110.

SEC. 195. A contract made by a district for the instruction of its pupils under the above provision, shall not be for a longer period than two years from the commencement of the term next following the making of such contract, and may at any time be modified by legislation; and nothing in such provision or contract shall be held to relieve a district from its obligation to provide for the instruction of all its legal pupils in the studies prescribed by law for the full time required.

1888, No. 9, sec. 111.

III. INSTRUCTION WHEN DISTRICT FAILS TO PROVIDE IT.

SEC. 196. The instruction of the legal pupils of a district in the studies prescribed by law shall be for two or more terms in each year, of which no term shall be less than eight weeks, and all of which shall amount to twenty-four weeks. If a district does not at least thirty-six weeks before the first day of April commence the first term of instruction, or does not at least twenty weeks before said date commence the second term of instruction, or if the full period of instruction required is not completed by the second term, does not at least ten weeks before said date commence a third term of instruction, or if said district after commencing either of said terms shall discontinue the same before the expiration of the time required, the instruction which the district so fails to provide may be secured in the manner hereinafter provided.

1888, No. 9, sec. 112, amended by 1890, No. 5, sec. 2.

SEC. 197. Any voter in said district may present to the selectmen of the town a petition in writing, setting forth the neglect of the district, and asking that instruction be provided. Upon receiving such petition, the selectmen shall fix a time and place for hearing thereon, and, if the district has elected officers, shall direct that said petition and notice of the time and place of hearing be served upon the prudential committee of the district, like a writ of summons, at least six days before the time of hearing.

1888, No. 9, sec. 113.

SEC. 198. At the time and place appointed, upon proof of notice to the committee, if notice was required, the selectmen shall proceed to a hearing, and if upon hearing they find the statements of the petition to be true, they shall forthwith declare the offices in the district vacant, if the district has elected officers, and shall make provision for the instruction of the legal pupils of the district, either in the district or elsewhere, at the times and for the length of time required, or for so much thereof as the district has failed to provide.

1888, No. 9, sec. 114.

SEC. 199. The selectmen may, without vote of the district, assess a tax upon the grand list of the district, sufficient to defray the expense of such instruction, including the expense of transportation if the pupils are sent out of the district, and shall make a rate-bill therefor. The town collector shall collect such tax, and in such collection shall have the same powers and be subject to the same liabilities as in the collection of town taxes. The moneys collected shall be paid to the selectmen, who shall defray therewith, and with any public moneys coming to said district, the expenses incurred as above provided.

1888, No. 9, sec. 115.

SEC. 200. If the instruction furnished by the selectmen, together with that furnished by the district, if any, before petition is made to the selectmen, amounts to the number of weeks required by law, such district shall be entitled to its share of the public moneys, notwithstanding the want of official certificates in the register.

1888, No. 9, sec. 116.

SEC. 201. A district may by vote provide a kindergarten school for the instruction of children under five years of age residing in the district; and when such a school is maintained it shall be attended by such pupils over five years of age as the prudential committee may designate.

1888, No. 9, sec. 151.

SEC. 202. For public school instruction in the branches prescribed by law, a pupil shall attend the school provided by the district in which he resides. The prudential committee of a district maintaining a school for advanced pupils may permit non-residents to attend such school upon the payment of reasonable tuition.

1888, No. 9, sec. 152.

SEC. 203. A district may by vote establish evening schools, and may maintain the same as day schools are maintained; and each session of an evening school may be treated as a half-day session of a public school.

1888, No. 9, sec. 165.

SEC. 203 a. The clerk of each school district shall annually, during the last two weeks of the school year, prepare an accurate list containing the name and age of each child of school age residing in the district, and the name of the parent or other person having control of such child; and he shall keep such list on file, and make such report therefrom as the superintendent of education may require.

1888, No. 9, sec. 103. See secs. 98 and 100.

CHAPTER XIV.

SCHOOL TAXES AND SCHOOL MONEY.

I. SCHOOL DISTRICT TAXES.

SECTION 204. The grand list of a school district shall be made up of the polls of inhabitants of the district, of the real estate lying in the district, and of the personal estate taxable therein ; and real estate shall be taxed for school purposes only in the district in which it is situated.

1888, No. 9, sec. 200.

SEC. 205. A school district may, by vote, raise a tax upon its list for the support of schools therein; and all expenses incurred by a district for the support of schools, in excess of public moneys received by the district, shall be so defrayed.

1888, No. 9, sec. 201.

SEC. 206. The prudential committee shall, as soon after such vote as circumstances may require, assess a tax for the amount voted to be raised, and make out a rate bill of the same; and any justice of a county in which the whole or part of such district is situated, shall, on application, make out a warrant directed to the district collector, authorizing and requiring him to levy and collect such tax within the time limited in such warrant, and pay the same to the treasurer of the district.

1888, No. 9, sec. 202.

SEC. 207. A district may by vote, at the meeting at which a tax is voted, direct the collector to deduct a per cent fixed by said vote, from the tax of a person who shall pay his tax before a day fixed by said vote. A collector shall make no deduction in favor of a person who does not pay his tax before the day fixed.

1888, No. 9, sec. 203.

SEC. 208. The collector of a tax from which deduction may be had as above provided, shall appoint a day within the time limited, and a place within the district, when and where he will attend to and receive such tax ; and shall post a notification thereof in three public places in the district, and publish the same in each newspaper printed in the district at least ten days before the time appointed ; and shall attend at the same time and place appointed to receive payment of such tax.

1888, No. 9, sec. 204.

SEC. 209. A district may, by a two-thirds vote, instruct the prudential committee to omit, in making up a tax-bill, the names of such persons as are unable to pay their proportion of the tax; and a district may by a two-thirds vote remit or make abatement on a tax-bill to an amount not exceeding five per cent of the same.

1888, No. 9, sec. 205.

SEC. 210. The officers of a school district, except the collector, shall be a board for the abatement of district taxes, and as such board shall have the powers which the board for the abatement of town taxes has in the abatement of town taxes. A majority of such officers shall constitute a quorum. The prudential committee, on request of the collector, shall call a meeting of said board in the month of March in each year, previous to the annual school meeting, by posting notice therefor in three public places in said district at least five days before such meeting.

1888, No 9, sec. 206, amended by 1890, No. 5, sec. 2.

SEC. 211. The district collector shall proceed in the same manner and have the same powers in levying and collecting district taxes, as town collectors in levying and collecting town taxes, and shall within the time limited collect and pay the same to the district treasurer; and the pruden-tial committee shall have the same authority to enforce the collection and payment of district taxes that town treasurers have to enforce the collection and payment of town taxes.

1888, No. 9, sec. 207.

SEC. 212. A district collector shall. on the written request of one of the prudential committee, pay to the district treasurer all moneys belonging to the district collected by him up to that time, and submit his taxbook and list to said Treasurer for inspection and computation; and if a collector shall neglect so to do for ten days after receiving such request,he shall forfeit to the district one hundred dollars, to be recovered in an action on this statue, and his office shall be vacant.

1888, No. 9, sec. 208.

SEC. 213. When a demand is made upon a school district for the payment of an execution issued against it, and the district has no available funds to pay the same, the prudential committee shall forthwith assess, and have collected, a tax sufficient to pay such execution and the charges and twelve per cent interest, in the same manner as a tax voted by the district is assessed and collected.

1888, No. 9, sec. 209.

II. TOWN SCHOOL TAXES.

SEC. 214. A town may at an annual meeting, or at a meeting warned for that purpose, raise money for the use of schools, by a tax on the list of such town.

1888, No. 9, sec. 227

SEC. 215. If in any year the income appropriated for the use of schools in a town, (excluding the income from the Huntington fund), with any tax voted by town, after deducting one-half the income of the United States deposit money, amounts to a less sum than twelve per cent of the grand list of the town, the selectmen shall draw an order on the town treasurer on or before the fifteenth day of March for such amount as such sum is less than such twelve per cent, for the use of schools in such town.

1888, No. 9, sec. 228, amended by 1890, No. 5, sec. 2.

SEC. 216. If the selectmen do not draw an order as provided in the preceding section, and appropriate the amount of such order for the support of schools as provided by law, the town shall forfeit to the county a sum equal to double the amount for which the selectmen are required to draw an order, to be recovered by information or indictment in the county court.

1888, No. 9, sec. 229.

SEC. 217. One-fourth of such penalty shall be for the use of the county, and three-fourths shall be paid to the selectmen for the use of schools in such towns; and the treasurer of the county, immediately after the receipt of such money, shall give notice thereof to the selectmen of the town, who shall forthwith receive, apportion and appropriate the same to the support of schools in such town, in the manner herein provided.

1888, No. 9, sec. 230.

SEC. 218. Grand juries shall annually inquire whether towns in their counties have appropriated and expended the required sum for the support of schools as provided in this chapter, and in case of neglect they shall present their indictment thereof to the court.

1888, No. 9, sec. 231.

SEC. 219. The town superintendent of schools shall learn if the requirements of this chapter relating to the appropriation and expenditure of moneys from the town treasury for the support of schools are complied with, and in case of a non-compliance he shall bring the matter to the attention of the State's attorney or grand jury.

1888, No. 9, sec. 232, amended by 1890, No. 5, sec. 2.

III. DIVISION OF PUBLIC MONEYS.

SEC. 220. The selectmen of such town shall annually, on the Friday next preceding the last Tuesday of March, divide the school moneys in the treasury of such town among the school districts in such town; and such moneys shall be paid over, under the direction of the selectmen, to the treasurers of the several districts.

1888, No. 9, sec. 233, amended by 1890, No. 5, sec. 2.

SEC. 221. A graded school district in a town having the town system shall receive from the public moneys of such town a share which shall bear such proportion to the whole amount of public moneys as the aggregate attendance in such district bears to the aggregate attendance of the whole town.

1888, No. 9, sec. 141, amended by 1892, No. 20, sec. 1.

SEC. 222. If the sum for division does not exceed twelve hundred dollars, one-half thereof: if such sum exceeds twelve hundred dollars and does not exceed twenty-four hundred dollars, one-half of the first twelve hundred dollars and one-sixth of the remainder: if such sum exceeds twenty-four hundred dollars and does not exceed thirty-six hundred dollars, one-half of the first twelve hundred dollars, one-sixth of the second twelve hundred dollars, and one-twelfth of the remainder; if such sum exceeds thirty-six hundred dollars, nine hundred dollars of such sum shall be divided among the school districts in each town equally, except as is otherwise provided in the case of districts only partially situated in the town.

1888, No. 9, sec. 234.

See sec. 120, ante.

SEC. 223.   The remainder of such moneys shall be divided among the districts in the town in proportion to the aggregate attendance of pupils between the ages of five and twenty years upon the schools of the district during the preceding school year, except as otherwise provided in the case of districts only partially situated in the town; such aggregate attendance to be ascertained from the records thereof kept in the registers of such schools by adding together the number of days of actual attendance of each pupil between the ages of five and eighteen years.

1888, No. 9, sec. 235.

SEC. 224.   Before making such division the selectmen shall carefully examine the entries in each register, and ascertain whether a school has been kept in the district twenty-four weeks during the school year, and whether it appears from the certificate of the prudential committee that such school was kept by teachers duly licensed; and whether the entries required to be made by the district clerk have been made as required; and no public money shall be distributed to a school district unless such district has supported a school twenty-four weeks during the school year; nor unless the register contains the certificate of the prudential committee as to the date and character of the certificates of the teachers, nor unless it appears from such certificates that such school was taught the entire twenty-four weeks by licensed teachers, nor unless the register has been properly filled out by the district clerk.

1888, No. 9, sec. 236.

SEC. 225.   The prudential committee, or if he is disabled from doing so, some other person having knowledge in the matter, shall on or before the first day of April in each year, return to the town clerk a statement under oath of the actual cash expenditure of the district for the preceding school year for school purposes other than the construction or repair of buildings; and no district shall be entitled to receive any portion of its school moneys unless such return is so made.   No district shall receive from the town the full amount of its school moneys unless it has actually expended during such preceding school year for school purposes, other than the construction or repair of buildings, a sum equal to the amount of its school moneys for such year, exclusive of private bequests, and one-tenth of its grand list for such preceding year, and the sum paid to a school district in any one year shall be diminished by the amount by which the sum actually so expended by the district in such preceding year, is less than the school moneys, exclusive of private bequests and one-tenth the grand list of the district for such preceding year.   And such difference instead of being paid to the district shall be distributed to the remaining school districts in town entitled to the same upon the aggregate attendance in such district.

1888, No. 9, sec. 237, amended by 1890, No. 5, sec. 2.

SEC. 226. When a district actually expends in any school year, in the maintenance of a legal public school, (for not more than twenty-four weeks), other than in the construction and repair of buildings, a sum greater than the amount of its school moneys for that year and one-third of its grand list, it shall receive from the town one-half of such excess, provided such expenditure be reasonable. And if the selectmen and prudential committee cannot agree as to this, the certificate of the town superintendent for the county [town] shall be final. Such excess shall be paid over by the town at the same time with the school moneys, or as soon thereafter as the certificate of the town superintendent is furnished.

1888, No. 9, sec. 238, amended by 1890, No. 5, sec. 2.

SEC. 227. A prudential committee who knowingly shall make a false certificate as to the date and character of teachers' certificates, or a false statement of the amount expended, or a district clerk who knowingly shall make false answers to the inquiries contained in the register, or a selectman who shall knowingly distribute public money to a school district not entitled thereto, shall forfeit to the town one hundred dollars, to be recovered in an action on this statute.

1888, No. 9, sec. 240.

SEC. 228. The town superintendent of schools shall annually make inquiry as to the division of the public money, and report to the town any violation of the requirements of the law.

1888, No. 9, sec. 241, amended by 1890, No. 5, sec. 2.

CHAPTER XV.

SCHOOL HOUSES.

SECTION 229. A school district may by vote raise a tax on its list to purchase or hire lands or buildings for school purposes, and to build, repair or furnish a school house, or as many school houses as may be needed for the schools of the district.

1888, No. 9, sec. 245.

SEC. 230. A school district may elect a special committee to purchase or hire lands or buildings for school purposes, or to superintend the building or repairing of a school house, or to procure necessary furniture and utensils therefor.

1888, No. 9, sec. 246.

SEC. 231. A prudential committee receiving a report from the town superintendent of schools recommending the repair or furnishing of a school house, and not complying with the recommendations in such report, shall cause such articles to be inserted in the notice of the next meeting of the district as will enable the district to act upon such recommendations.

1888, No. 9, sec. 247, amended by 1890, No. 5, sec. 2.

SEC. 232. A district taking measures to provide a building to be occupied as a school house, as authorized in section two hundred and forty-five, [Section 229], may, at the same meeting, by a two-thirds vote, determine the location of the school house.

1888, No. 9, sec. 248.

SEC. 233. If the district fails to agree upon such location, the selectmen of the town or towns in which such district is situated may, upon application of the prudential committee, determine such location.

1888, No. 9, sec. 249.

SEC. 234. If the prudential committee neglects for five days to apply to the selectmen, three voters of the district may apply in writing to such selectmen, stating the neglect of the prudential committee, and petitioning the selectmen to fix upon a location.

1888, No. 9, sec. 250.

SEC. 235. The selectmen so applied to, shall forthwith give notice of a hearing, in the same manner as school district meetings are warned, and shall hear the petitioners and persons interested; and if the failure of the district to determine a location, and of the prudential committee to apply within the limited time appears at such hearing, the selectmen shall determine such location, and shall make return of the application and of their doings thereon to the district clerk, who shall record the same.

1888, No. 9, sec. 251.

SEC. 236. If a district neglects for two years to provide suitable school-houses, or neglects for one year to make the repairs or do the furnishing recommended by the town superintendent of schools, application for an order in the matter may be made by two voters of the district to the selectmen of the town or towns in which the district is situated.

1888, No. 9, sec. 252, amended by 1890, No. 5, sec. 2.

SEC. 237. Such selectmen shall appoint a time and place for hearing the applicants and persons interested, and shall cause the applicants to give notice to such district of such application, and of the time and place of hearing, which notice shall be served upon the district like a writ of summons, at least twenty days before the time appointed for hearing.

1888, No. 9, sec. 253.

SEC. 238. If it appears on hearing that the district is guilty of the neglect charged, and that the interests of education in the district require an order in the matter, the selectmen shall order the district to provide a school house, or to make the repairs or do the furnishing recommended by the town superintendent as the case may be, which order shall be served on the district like ordinary process in civil causes.

1888, No. 9, sec. 254, amended by 1890, No. 5, sec. 2.

SEC. 239. If the district fails to comply with such order within six months after service thereof, the selectmen who made the order, or their successors in office, shall provide the school-house, or make the repairs or do the furnishing required by their order ; and when providing a school-house, they shall provide suitable out-buildings and grounds therefor.

1888, No. 9, sec. 255.

SEC. 240. The selectmen may assess a tax upon the district list for the amount required for the purposes aforesaid, and make out a rate bill therefor ; and said tax shall be collected by the collector of the town in which the school-house is located, in the same manner as town taxes are collected, and shall be paid to the selectmen and be used by them for the purposes aforesaid.

1888, No. 9, sec. 256.

SEC. 241. The proceedings under the five preceding sections shall be recorded in the office of the clerk of the town in which the school-house is located, and copies of such record, certified by such clerk, shall be evidence in the courts.

1888, No. 9, sec. 257.

SEC. 242. When it devolves upon the selectmen to locate or build a school-house, if a majority of such selectmen cannot agree upon a location therefor, they shall forthwith make a return of the application made to them and of their failure to agree, to the district clerk, who shall make a

record of the same. In such case three voters of the district may apply in
writing to an assistant judge of the county court to determine the location of such school-house ; and such judge shall give notice of a hearing,
hear, determine the matter, and make return of his proceedings, and such
proceedings shall be recorded, as provided in case of the location of a
school-house by selectmen; and the assistant judge shall for his services
be paid by the district three dollars a day and his expenses.

1888, No. 9, sec. 258.

SEC. 243. When a school-house is located and lands for such school-
house and yards are needed, or when a district votes to purchase additional land for school purposes, if the owner of such lands refuses to convey the same to the district for a reasonable price, the selectmen of the
town or towns in which the district is situated, on the application of the
prudential committee, shall locate and set out the necessary lands and
cause the same to be surveyed; and shall appoint a time and place for a
hearing and give notice thereof to persons interested in the land to be
taken, either personally or by written notice left at the residence of the
owner or occupant of such land; and at such hearing shall ascertain the
damages sustained by such interested persons; and the damages assessed
shall be paid or tendered to such persons before taking possession of the
land.

1888, No. 9, sec. 259.

SEC. 244. When the selectmen decide to take land, they shall in their
order for that purpose, fix a time and notify the owner or occupant thereof, within which he will be required to remove his buildings, fences,
timber, wood, trees and wall, which, in case of inclosed or improved land,
shall not, without the consent of the owner, be less than three months, nor
until the compensation for damages to such land is tendered or paid; and
if they are not removed within that time, the selectmen shall remove
them at the expense of said district; but the district shall not take possession of such land until the damages agreed upon or as determined by the
selectmen shall have been paid or tendered to the persons entitled thereto.

1888, No. 9, sec. 260.

SEC. 245. All orders and proceedings of the selectmen, under the
provisions of the two preceding sections, with the survey of the land
taken, shall be recorded in the town clerk's office of the town in which the
land lies.

1888, No. 9, sec. 261.

SEC. 246. If the owner of such land does not accept the damages
awarded by the selectmen, the prudential committee of the district may

agree with him to refer the question of damages to one or more disinterested persons, whose award shall be made in writing, and shall be final.

1888, No. 9, sec. 262.

SEC. 247. If a person interested in such land is dissatisfied with such location or with the damages awarded by the selectmen, he may apply by petition to the county court at its next stated term, if there is sufficient time for notice, and if not, to the succeeding term; and any number of persons aggrieved may join in the petition. The petition, with a citation, shall be served on one of the prudential committee of the school district, at least twelve days before the session of the court, and the court shall appoint three disinterested commissioners who shall determine the amount of damages sustained by the persons interested therein.

1888, No. 9, sec. 263.

SEC. 248. The commissioners shall give six days' notice to one of the prudential committee of the school district of the time and place of making such inquiry and hearing the parties; and on the report of the commissioners the court shall render judgment for the petitioner to recover against the school district such damages as appear to be just, and may tax costs as seems just for either party, and award execution in the premises.

1888, No. 9, sec. 264.

SEC. 249. If lands so required by a school district are encumbered by mortgage, the school district shall cause the same notice to be given to the mortgagee, or the assignee of the mortgage, required to be given to the owner; and the damage agreed upon, or otherwise determined, as specified in this chapter, shall be paid to the mortgagee or his assignee; but if the sum due on the mortgage is less than the damage, the amount due on the mortgage shall be paid to the holder, and the balance to the owner.

1888, No. 9, sec. 265.

SEC. 250. When the damages finally awarded for lands so taken by a school district are paid to the persons entitled thereto, a valid title to such lands shall vest in the district for the purposes aforesaid.

1888, No. 9, sec. 266.

SEC. 251. A school district may, by a two-thirds vote, if such vote represents a majority of the grand list of the district, sell its school-house and the land connected therewith; and the names of those voting for the sale shall be taken and recorded.

1888, No. 9, sec. 267.

PART III.

Miscellaneous Provisions Relating to Public Instruction and the Care and Preservation of School Property.

CHAPTER XVI.

INSTRUCTION OF THE DEAF, DUMB, BLIND, IDIOTIC AND FEEBLE—MINDED.

SECTION 252.   The governor shall be by virtue of his office commissioner of the deaf, dumb and blind, and of the idiotic and feeble-minded children of indigent parents, and as such commissioner shall constitute the board for their instruction.

R. L. sec. 680.

SEC. 253.   He shall annually report to the legislature his proceedings under this chapter with an account of the expenditures arising therefrom, and shall receive fifty dollars annually for his services as such commissioner.

R. L. sec. 681.

SEC. 254.   A sum not exceeding five thousand dollars is annually appropriated for the benefit of the deaf and dumb, and a sum not exceeding four thousand dollars for the benefit of the blind, and a sum not exceeding two thousand dollars for the benefit of the idiotic and feeble-minded children of indigent parents, to be used agreeably to the provisions of this chapter.

R. L. sec. 682.

SEC. 255. Until provision is otherwise made by law the beneficiaries mentioned in this chapter shall be instructed at the following places: The deaf and dumb at the American Asylum for the education of the deaf and dumb at Hartford, Connecticut, or the Clark Institution at Northampton, Massachusetts; the blind at the New England Institution for the instruction of the blind at Boston, Massachusetts ; and the idiotic and feeble-minded children at the Massachusetts school for idiotic and feeble-minded youth, at Boston, or at such other institutions of like nature as the above, situate in New England, as the governor shall select.

R. L. sec. 683, amended by 1892, No. 27, sec. 1.

SEC. 256. The board of civil authority in each town shall ascertain, and certify to the county clerk on or before the first day of February annually, the number of deaf and dumb persons and the number of blind persons in such town, their ages, conditions and circumstances, and the ability of their parents to educate them, the names of all idiotic and feeble-minded children between the ages of five and fourteen years residing in such town and the pecuniary ability and circumstances of their parents or the persons bound to support them, and whether in the opinion of such board the persons enumerated and named are proper subjects for the charity of the State, and whether they and their parents or guardians are willing they should become beneficiaries of either of the institutions mentioned in the preceding section, or such other institution as is provided by law for the instruction of such persons.

R. L. sec. 684.

SEC. 257. Each county clerk shall make return to the governor, before the first day of March in each year, of the information he receives from the several boards of civil authority in his county.

R. L. sec. 685.

SEC. 258. The governor may designate beneficiaries, as aforesaid, may direct the auditor of accounts to draw orders on the treasury for any part of the appropriations provided in section five hundred ninety-five [sec. 682] [sec. 254, ante] ; may superintend and direct all concerns relating to the education of deaf, dumb, blind, idiotic, or feeble-minded persons, inhabitants of the State, and may allow all or any portion of the expenses of their conveyance to, and support in, the institutions in which they are instructed for such time as he deems proper; and he may in his discretion take bonds to indemnify the State against expenses which accrue in consequence of the' sickness, clothing, or transportation of any beneficiary.

R. L. sec. 686.

SEC. 259. The selectmen of the several towns in this State are hereby authorized and empowered to execute in their official capacity in behalf of their respective towns, without a previous vote of said town for that purpose, the bond which may be required to be given by the town to indemnify the State against expenses which may accrue in consequence of the sickness, clothing or transportation of the deaf, dumb and blind State beneficiaries from such town.

R. L. sec. 687.

SEC. 260. When a person is designated a beneficiary, the town in which he resides shall defray the expenses of his conveyance to and from the institution in which he is to be instructed if in the opinion of the selectmen his parent or guardian is not able to pay the same.

R. L. sec. 688.

SEC. 261. The governor may designate one or more beneficiaries, under the provisions of chapter forty-one of the Revised Laws [chapter sixteen of this compilation], relating to the instruction of the blind and appropriating money therefor, who may receive their education within this State, when, in his judgment, adequate advantages exist for the proper instruction of such person, or persons, and the public ·good would be subserved thereby, notwithstanding such beneficiary, or beneficiaries, may be beyond the age of sixteen years.

1884, No. 39, sec. 1.

SEC. 262. Such beneficiary, or beneficiaries, shall each be entitled to receive the same annual share of the general appropriation for this purpose as is paid by the State for the support and education of a single scholar at the New England Institution for the Instruction of the Blind at Boston, Massachusetts, which allowance shall continue for such time as the governor may deem reasonable and necessary, and shall be paid to such beneficiary, or beneficiaries, as provided in section six hundred and eighty-six of the Revised Laws, and in quarterly installments, upon the certificate of the selectmen of the town where such person or persons may reside, that a proper and sufficient course of study has been pursued.

1884, No. 39, sec. 2.

CHAPTER XVII.

OFFENSES AND PENALTIES.

I. PENALTY FOR DISTURBING SCHOOLS.

SECTION 263. A person who by a disorderly or unlawful act disturbs a town, society or district meeting, or a school, or any meeting lawfully assembled, or by force or menace interrupts the business of such meeting or school, shall be fined not more than one hundred dollars.

R. L., sec. 4229.

SEC. 264. A person over ten years of age not connected with the school who annoys or disturbs a school by remaining at or near it, or by not departing on request of the teacher or prudential committee, [or school directors], shall be fined not more than twenty dollars. Justices shall have jurisdiction of offenses under this section.

R. L., sec. 4230.
See sec. 69, ante.

II. PENALTY FOR DEFACING SCHOOL BUILDINGS, INJURING TREES OR TRESPASSING UPON GROUNDS.

SEC. 265. A person who wilfully and maliciously breaks a door or window of, or otherwise injures, a dwelling house or other building, whether occupied or not, or a sign thereon, or a fence or wall, not being his own property, or disfigures the same with paint or otherwise, or defaces the same by writing, printing or painting thereon any obscene word, figures or devices, shall be fined not more than twenty dollars or imprisoned not more than ninety days, or both ; and the offender shall also be liable to pay the owner of the property injured the damages occasioned, in an action on this statute with full costs.

R. L., sec. 4199.

SEC. 266.   A person who carelessly and without malice injures or defaces any part of a building belonging to a town or county, or the appurtenances thereof, or any public building, hall or room, by cutting, writing, marking, standing in the windows, or in any other manner, or injures the furniture, fence, yard, posts, grounds, shade trees or shrubbery connected with such building, or fastens a horse or other animal to the fence, posts or trees about such building or posts bills, placards and notices upon such building or its appurtenances or upon the fence or trees belonging to the same, whereby any defacement results, shall forfeit to the State not less than two dollars, with full costs, to be recovered in the name of the State on complaint of a grand juror of the town or the State's attorney for the county.

R. L., sec. 4200.

SEC. 267.   A person who injures a shade or ornamental tree or shrub standing upon the grounds belonging to a school house or academy, by cutting or breaking the same, or by fastening a horse or other animal to the same, shall be subject to the penalties and liabilities provided in section 4199 [sec. 265].

R. L. sec. 4204.

III.   PENALTY FOR EMBEZZLEMENT OF SCHOOL FUNDS.

SEC. 268.   A person entrusted with the charge of money, land or other property belonging to a town or school district for the use of schools, who embezzles, misapplies, or conceals the same or any part thereof shall be liable to be removed from his trust and shall forfeit to such town or district, as the case may be, double the amount so embezzled, misapplied or concealed, to be recovered in an action on the case in the name of such town or district, with costs.

R. L., sec. 4152.

IV.   PENALTY FOR CARRYING CONCEALED WEAPONS.

SEC. 269.   A person who shall carry or have in his possession while a member of and in attendance upon any school, any firearms, dirk knife, bowie knife, dagger, or other dangerous or deadly weapon, shall, upon conviction thereof, be fined not exceeding twenty dollars.

1892, No. 85, sec. 2.

V.   FENCES AROUND SCHOOL HOUSE YARDS.

SEC. 270.   No barbed wire fence shall be built or maintained around any school house yard.

1892, No. 104, sec. 1.

SEC. 271. Any person offending against the provisions of this act [sec. 270] shall be fined not less than twenty dollars nor more than fifty dollars.

1892, No. 104, sec. 2.

[NOTE.—Sections 270 and 271 are in force after May 1st, 1892.]

CHAPTER XVIII.

APPROPRIATIONS IN AID OF COLLEGES AND TO ESTABLISH SCHOLARSHIPS THEREIN.

SECTION
272. $6,000 appropriated annually in aid of the University of Vermont and State Agricultural College; $3,600 to be used in furnishing instruction in the industrial arts; $2,400 to be used in providing for thirty scholarships; senators to designate students; vacancies, how filled; when appointments to be made.
273. $2,400 appropriated annually in aid of Middlebury College to be use in providing thirty scholarships; appointments, how made.
274. Trustees may fill vacancies, on failure of senator to appoint.

SECTION
275 Preference to candidates for agricultural and industrial department; proviso.
276. $2400, appropriated annually for providing thirty scholarships in Norwich University; appointments how made; vacancies.
277. Senators failing to make appointments or fill vacancies, trustees to do so.
278. Moneys paid to said University to be kept in a separate account.
279. Laws inconsistent with this act repealed.

SECTION 272. The auditor of accounts is hereby directed to draw his order on the State treasurer in favor of the treasurer of the University of Vermont and State Agricultural College, semi-annually on the first day of December and June, for the sum of three thousand dollars, of which sum of six thousand dollars per annum the sum of thirty-six hundred dollars shall be expended by said institution in providing instruction in branches related to the industrial arts; and the sum of twenty-four hundred dollars in paying the tuition and incidental college charges of thirty students therein, one of whom shall be designated and appointed by each senator in the General Assembly, such appointment to be made by such senator from his respective county, provided any suitable candidate shall apply therefor, otherwise from any county in the State, and all vacancies in such appointments shall be filled by the senator who made the appointment vacated, or by his successor in office; said appointments to be made in the month of June preceding the commencement of the college course of the student so appointed, and whenever such vacancy shall occur.

1892, No. 25, sec. 1.

SEC. 273. The auditor of accounts is further directed to draw his order on the State treasurer in favor of the treasurer of Middlebury College semi-annually on the first day of December and June for the sum of twelve hundred dollars, said sum of twenty-four hundred dollars annually to be expended by said college in providing thirty scholarships under the same conditions named in section one of this act [sec. 263] governing the appointments to thirty scholarships in the University of Vermont and State Agricultural College.

1892, No. 25, sec. 2.

SEC. 274. Whenever any senator from any county shall fail to make an original appointment or to fill any vacancy among such appointed students after one month's notice of his right to do so from the president of either of such institutions, the trustees may make such appointment or fill such vacancy by appointments from that county, if there are any applicants therefrom who shall pass the examination required by the rules of said institution, and if not, then from any county in the State.

1892, No. 25, sec. 3.

SEC. 275. Senators from any county shall in their appointment of candidates for scholarships in the University of Vermont and State Agricultural College give preference to the candidates for the agricultural and industrial department; but if at any time there are not thirty suitable applicants for said department, then said senators may appoint to any other department of said college.

1892, No. 25, sec. 4.

SEC. 276. The auditor of accounts is hereby directed to draw his order on the State treasurer, in favor of the treasurer of Norwich University semi-annually on the first day of December and June for the sum of twelve hundred dollars, said sum of twenty-four hundred dollars annually to be expended by said University in payment of the tuition and room rent of thirty students therein, one of whom shall be designated and appointed by each senator in the General Assembly, such appointment to be made by such senator from his respective county, provided any suitable candidate shall apply therefor, otherwise from any county in the State, and all vacancies in such appointments shall be filled by the senator who made the appointment vacated, or by his successor in office. Said appointment to be made in the month of June preceding the commencement of the college course of the student so appointed, and whenever such vacancy shall occur.

1892, No. 26, sec. 1.

SEC. 277. Whenever any senator from any county shall fail to make an original appointment or to fill any vacancy among such appointed students after one month's notice of his right to do so from the president of said university, the trustees may make such appointment or fill such vacancy, by appointment from that county if there are any applicants therefrom who shall pass the examination required by the rules of said institution, and if not, then from any county in the State.

1892, No. 26, sec. 2.

SEC. 278. All moneys in any wise paid to said university or the students thereof by the State or its quartermaster-general shall be kept in a separate and independent account.

1892, No. 26, sec. 3.

SEC. 279. All previous acts or parts of facts relating to scholarships in Norwich University are hereby repealed.

1892, No. 26, sec. 4.

CHAPTER XIX.

REGISTRATION—DUTIES OF SCHOOL OFFICERS.

SECTION 280. The school district clerks in each town, or in towns not divided into districts, the clerk of the school board, shall annually, in the month of January, ascertain the births and deaths which occurred in their respective districts, during the year next preceding the first day of January and shall report to the town clerk on or before the first day of February, the date and place of birth of each child, its name and sex, the names and residence of its parents, and the occupation of the father. They shall also report the date, place and disease or apparent cause of each death, the name and sex of the deceased, whether married or single, his age in years, months and days, place of birth, the name of his parents and his occupation if over fifteen years of age.

R. L. sec. 2547.

SEC. 281. If a district clerk or clerk of school board fails to make the required return or makes an incomplete or incorrect return, he shall forfeit all compensation therefor and be fined not less than five dollars; and the town clerk shall forthwith cause prosecution to be commenced against him in the name of the State to recover such penalty.

R. L. sec. 2548.

SEC. 282. So much of this chapter as relates to the duties of school district clerks in collecting and making returns of births and deaths shall not apply to the city of Burlington.

R. L. sec. 2549.

SEC. 283. Town clerks shall carefully examine the returns of births and deaths made to them by the clerks of the several school districts; and if the returns are made up and returned agreeably to law, they shall furnish the school district clerk so complying with the requirements of law a certificate to that effect; and on presentation of such certificate to the selectmen, they shall draw an order on the town treasurer to pay such school district clerk or clerk of school board, fifteen cents for each birth or death returned.

R. L. sec. 2550.

INDEX

TO THE

Compiled School Laws.

.

www.ingramcontent.com/pod-product-compliance
Lightning Source LLC
Chambersburg PA
CBHW031451270326
41930CB00007B/953